T0130406

THE
Busy Butterfly

H F CANTRELL

Copyright © 2020 H F Cantrell.

All rights reserved. No part of this book may be used or reproduced by any means, graphic, electronic, or mechanical, including photocopying, recording, taping or by any information storage retrieval system without the written permission of the author except in the case of brief quotations embodied in critical articles and reviews.

Balboa Press books may be ordered through booksellers or by contacting:

Balboa Press
A Division of Hay House
1663 Liberty Drive
Bloomington, IN 47403
www.balboapress.com
1 (877) 407-4847

Because of the dynamic nature of the Internet, any web addresses or links contained in this book may have changed since publication and may no longer be valid. The views expressed in this work are solely those of the author and do not necessarily reflect the views of the publisher, and the publisher hereby disclaims any responsibility for them.

Any people depicted in stock imagery provided by Getty Images are models, and such images are being used for illustrative purposes only.
Certain stock imagery © Getty Images.

Interior Image Credit: H F Cantrell

ISBN: 978-1-9822-5044-7 (sc)
ISBN: 978-1-9822-5043-0 (e)

Print information available on the last page.

Balboa Press rev. date: 07/17/2020

INTRODUCTION

FIELD GUIDE BOOK

There are hundreds of butterflies, and they occur in many parts of the world. There are several books or guides for identifying butterflies. I use "Kaufman Field Guide to Butterflies of North America". It is restricted to North America and does not include regions of the world beyond North America. To completely review the entire Kaufman book is beyond the scope of this book. In summary, Kaufman has listed 18 groups of butterflies throughout North America. Within these 18 groups are sub-groups that share similar characteristics. The number of butterflies in a sub-group ranges from 3 or 4 up to 28. This accounts for the hundreds of butterflies throughout North America. The Kaufman book contains descriptions of the groups and sub-groups of hundreds of butterflies as well as a small map showing the region where the butterflies have been found. Some sub-groups of the larger group are found just in a specific region. Other groups inhabit most of the United States according to the maps in the Kaufman book. When attempting to identify a butterfly in your area, it is a good practice to refer to a guidebook map of the suspected group to check on whether it has been identified in your area of the United States.

Since there are many different butterflies in North America, this specific book will use those seen in this area of South Carolina to illustrate as many kinds of butterflies as possible. In our yard. We planted several "Butterfly Gardens" to attract butterflies to pollinate our vegetable plants that require pollination to produce fruits (beans, squash, tomatoes, etc.).

This book is not a complete treatment of all butterflies, rather it is an example of butterflies found in our area.

FLOWER PARTS

People of all ages enjoy watching butterflies visiting flowers. The butterflies appear to always be busy, flying from flower to flower. Their secret is they are searching for food from nectar in the flowers.

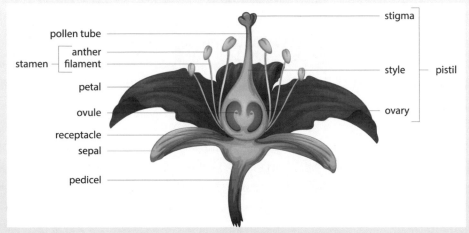

Image of a red flower, with parts labeled

Source: Getty Images

The butterfly visits the flower to take the nectar as food. In the process, pollen is transferred from the Anther to the Stigma and the pollen "fertilizes" the Ovary after it passes through the Style of the flower. A seed or later a fruit if formed after the fertilization process.

An actual flower showing parts of a flower.

Source: My photo

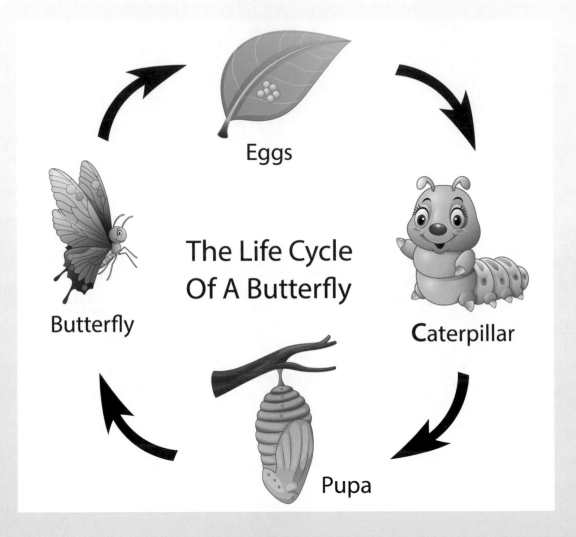

Source: Getty Images

The butterfly lays eggs on a leaf, time passes and a caterpillar hatches from the egg, the caterpillar forms a covering (Chrysalis or Cacoon) and time passes and a butterfly emerges from the Chrysalis and begins life as a butterfly. The cycle repeats in nature and we have more butterflies.

Image of a flower garden behind a rock wall

The following pages include pictures taken by me of the butterflies that visited our "Butterfly Gardens" during the summer of 2019.

Image of a white butterfly

The first example is the Whites. This a small butterfly, often referred to as **The Cabbage Butterfly**. It flies around rapidly and visits flowers for short periods of time. It also visits cabbage plants in vegetable gardens.

Image of a yellow butterfly

The next group is The **Sulphur**. These butterflies resemble the Whites and are sometimes grouped with them in books. Their color has a light greenish yellow. They are similar in size to the Whites and may be hard to distinguish from a distance. They resemble the Whites in their flight pattern also.

The Swallowtails group is common in our area and frequently seen around flowers. Their color and markings are well known with bright yellow and black patterns.

The **Longtails** are a unique butterfly. They get their name from the long tail they possess. They are basically black with light markings on the wings. In our area, they were rare, but interesting.

The **Dark Swallowtails** or **Spicebush Swallowtails** are another group that is seen in much of the Eastern United States. The contrasting colors make these butterflies another favorite.

Images of orange colored butterflies

These orange butterflies, with dark markings are either **Coppers** or **Metal Marks** or **Fritillaries** butterflies. These are less common than Swallowtails in our area. The Coppers and Metal Marks are not shown on the map as very abundant in our area of South Carolina. Only a few Fritillaries are shown on the map for this area. This fact demonstrates the difficulty of identifying these butterflies easily. Other butterflies are easier to identify.

Images of orange butterflies

Coppers or Metal Marks or Fritillaries

Images of bluish and black butterflies

These beautiful dark blue or black butterflies are most likely to be another variant of **Swallowtails.** That is the best match in the Kaufman field guide. This is another example of the difficulty in identification.

Dark Swallowtails

Image of a smallish butterfly

These small butterflies were less common in our garden. The brown with white spots color on this butterfly most closely resembles a **Skipper**

Image of a small yellow butterfly on a yellow flower

The small yellow butterfly on the yellow flower is hard to identify but resembles a **Sulphur.**

Images of primarily orange butterflies with dark markings

These beautiful butterflies are the **Monarchs**. They are some of the most beautiful of all the butterflies that visit our garden. They are easy to identify based on their colors and markings. They are also a favorite of many gardeners.

Monarchs

Butterfly Facts:

1. According to Kaufman's Field Guide, there are eighteen major groups of North American butterflies.
2. Each of the major groups is divided into subgroups according to their body traits, markings, color and geographic distribution. Some groups are found throughout North America. The subgroups are often more localized according to the geographical distribution. For example, the Alpine subgroups are found in different area of Northern Canada and Alaska.
3. According to Kaufman's book, one must consider a variety of traits to identify a specific butterfly. These include:
   a. Size
   b. Shape
   c. Posture
   d. Flight Style
   e. Fine Details
   f. Variation
   g. Habitat/Season
   h. Maps of Distribution

4. Locating butterflies

   Not all butterflies swarm to flowers, as seen in the photos of my butterfly garden. Some may be found in damp places. Others are attracted to rotting fruits or the sap of some plants or even animal feces. Some fly to hilltops to scout for other butterflies in order to mate, while some frequent trails or paths for search for a mate. Finally, some remain close to plants to ensure that the larvae can find food after they hatch from eggs.

   The study of butterflies becomes more interesting when you learn more about the many types and appreciate the many factors that describe their life. Regardless of where you live in North America, you are likely to discover butterflies nearby and with the help of a Field Guide you can discover the joy of watching them and learning more about these beautiful members of nature.

Butterflies collecting nectar.

Butterflies collecting nectar.

Printed in the United States
By Bookmasters